Copyright © 2022 by Carlos F. Peña

Published by Led to Lead, Inc.
Printed in the United States of Americ

All rights reserved. No part of this publication may be reproduced, distributed, or transmitted in any form or by any means, including photocopying, recording, or other electronic or mechanical methods, without the prior written permission of the publisher, except in the case of brief quotations embodied in critical reviews and certain other noncommercial uses permitted by copyright law. Published by Led to Lead®

Paperback ISBN: 978-0-578-38330-9

Ordering Information:
FX3 Ministries, Inc. books may be purchased in bulk. Special discounts are available on quantity purchases by corporations, associations, and others. Orders by U.S. trade bookstores and wholesalers. For details, contact the publisher at the address listed below. For permission requests, write to the publisher, addressed to:
Attention:
   Permissions
   FX3 Ministries
   13611 S. Dixie Hwy #463
   Miami, FL 33176
   www.faithfirefury.com

Italics in Scripture quotations are the author's emphasis.

Unless otherwise indicated, Scripture quotations are from:
The Holy Bible, English Standard Version (ESV)
© 2001 by Crossway Bibles, a division of Good News Publishers.
Used by permission. All rights reserved.

Other Scripture quotations are from:
The Holy Bible, New International Version (NIV)
© 1973, 1978, 1984, 2011 by Biblica, Inc.™
Used by permission. All rights reserved worldwide.
The Holy Bible, King James Version (KJV)

1st Edition, February 2022

Cover Design: Carlos F. Peña
Cover Photography: *Raw Pixel* / © *U.S. Government*

FX3 CHALLENGE
— FURY —

A 30-DAY STUDY ON HOW TO PASSIONATELY PURSUE WHAT GOD WANTS YOU TO DO

CARLOS F. PEÑA

LED TO LEAD

I dedicate this book to my Lord and Savior, Jesus Christ, and his incredible grace to transform this wayward man into a warrior for my wife and three awesome boys.

Also, to the brotherhood of men who I walk with and those I have yet to meet.

TABLE OF CONTENTS:

WHAT TO EXPECT	8
GROUP RULES	9
COMMITMENTS	11
THE THREE TENETS	12
SESSION 1: THE ARMOR	15
TRUTH	16
RIGHTEOUSNESS	19
PEACE	22
FAITH	25
SALVATION	28
SESSION 2: THE WARRIOR WAY	36
PRAYER	47
FELLOWSHIP	50
WITNESS TO THE WORLD	53
GODS FURIOUS LOVE	56
SESSION 3: THE FX3 BROTHERHOOD	59
THE LONE WOLF IS A LIE	61
BROTHERHOOD	64
STRENGTH	67
ENCOURAGEMENT	73
LOVE	79
SESSION 4: REFLECT & REVIEW	82
WRITE DAILY DIRECTIVES	83
MEMORY VERSES	109

Congratulations again on completing Phase Two, FX3 Fire. You're now ready to complete the challenge with FX3 Fury. In this final phase, you'll learn what it means and how to passionately pursue what God wants you to do.

HOW TO GET THE MOST OUT OF THE NEXT 30 DAYS.

In life, nothing worthwhile comes easy. Lasting change and transformation takes deliberate effort and time. This reality means that you need both **commitment and consistency** to see results.

These two factors are essential for advancement in any area of your life, especially when embarking on a spiritual growth journey. Miraculous things will happen when you commit to Jesus and the Holy Spirit. God will work in your life to accomplish His will for you. Considering this, the goal for you during these next thirty days is to:

- Learn what the spiritual armor is and how to use it.
- Unpack and live according to the FX3 Warrior code.
- Discover the strength and power that comes from the brotherhood.
- Apply Faith, Fire, and Fury to live a fulfilling and purposeful life!

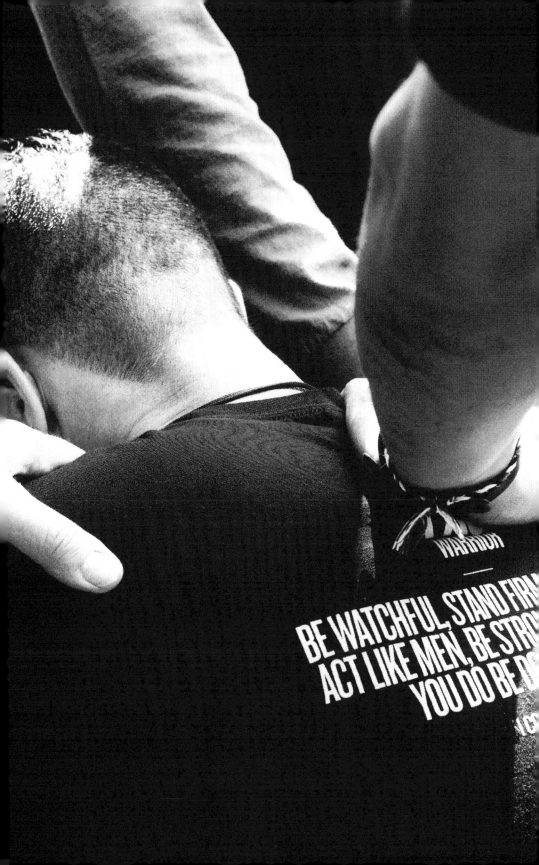

WHAT TO EXPECT

Before we start, we need to set some initial ground rules and expectations. Adhering to these guidelines will secure the health and growth of yourself and others when taking this journey with a fellow brother or in a group. It will also prevent any potential misunderstandings. But, more importantly, it provides you with focus and direction.

GROUP RULES

RESPECT:
Avoid dismissing others' thoughts, don't laugh at others when they've shared (unless it's a joke), and no put-downs of any kind. Opening up can be hard enough, and this place should be a welcoming place for all to find answers and support. Also, agreeing to disagree on specific points of view. Discussions are about discovery. If a conflict should arise, discuss the issue outside of group time on a one-on-one basis.

CONFIDENTIALITY:
Unfortunately, the saying "What happens in Vegas stays in Vegas" doesn't always prove true. Not the case for this brotherhood. What's said in the group stays in the group. No one wants to find out he has been the subject of gossip or well-meaning "prayer discussions." Violation of this trust is grounds for removal from the group.

LISTEN AND SUPPORT:
We care for one another during the discussions by really listening to what others are sharing. Try to avoid thinking about how you will respond or what you are going to say next. We're not here to "fix" or "rescue" each other. That's Jesus Christ's job through the power of the Holy Spirit. Instead, we listen for the Holy Spirit to provide opportunities to speak into each one of us and let him do the necessary work.

ACCOUNTABILITY:
Similar to listening and support, we approach accountability as the ability to help our brother accomplish his goals as it aligns with God's will. We're not to pass judgment or "shame" someone for falling short. Instead, we help them up, encourage them and remind them of what they are committed to doing.

JOHN 15:13

Greater love has no one than this, that someone lay down his life for his friends.

COMMITMENTS

1. For these next thirty days, I will make **my quiet time with God a priority** by making it the first thing I do in the morning. I will also partner up with a fellow brother and **check in with him regularly.** We will encourage and hold each other accountable. It could be as simple as a text, prayer, call, coffee, etc.

2. I will complete the **Daily Directives and memorize** the weekly memory verse. There are five Daily Directives per week, and *Create Your Own* days. *Create Your Own* days are for me to create my own devotional. Finally, I will complete the three action items for each Daily Directive which are:

Read: Although I may be busy, I will make time for God first, knowing all other things will align. Like food for the body, spiritual food is God's word. Therefore, at the very least, I will read the verse of the day.

Pray: I will also make time to pray as it's essential to my soul. When I pray, I will take a posture of humility and become receptive to hear God's voice and prompting. Consistency is key.

Meditate / Make It Real: I will get the most from my reading and prayer time by journaling my responses to the questions and verses. Journaling makes my thoughts tangible and actionable. I will also track my progress by checking the boxes for each Daily Directive to hold myself accountable and celebrate my accomplishments.

Share: I learn most when I teach what I learned. For this reason, I will take deliberate steps and time to share with others what God is saying to me through my studies.

3. I will come **prepared and ready to share** with my brother or within a group every week. I know the Spirit moves greatest when all of us contribute. I will complete the readings before meeting so that I and others will benefit the most from our time together.

Name: _____ Signature: _____

THE THREE TENETS

Based on 1 Cor. 16:13-14 and expanded upon in the book Faith Fire Fury, an FX3 Warrior lives out his life according to the following three tenets:

Faith: *We believe with complete confidence in God's inerrant Word. We treasure its truths, and respect its reproofs.* We acknowledge the Creator God as our heavenly Father, infinitely perfect and intimately acquainted with all our ways.

We place our hope on the fact that Christ died for our sins, then rose from the dead. Before God, he now declares us to be righteous and new creations. Christ's sacrifice on our behalf demands that we pursue a lifelong process of sanctification through the Spirit.

Fire: *We use our time, talents, gifts, and resources to live every day in a way that glorifies God.* We rely on the Holy Spirit and the Word to empower and continually transform us into the likeness of Christ. To do this, we study His word in depth to apply his teachings to our life.

We believe and accept that our identity and purpose are found in God's word and rely on the Spirit for guidance, empowerment, instruction, and correction.

Fury: *We passionately pursue what God wants us to do. We individually and collectively live sacrificially for others by sharing Christ's love, hope, and message of salvation with the world, and to help others to do the same.*

We're in a spiritual war with forces working against us, trying to prevent us from fulfilling our mission. To be victorious, we individually and collectively fight these battles under God's leadership, according to his word and his example.

For centuries, soldiers have used armor to protect themselves against the weapons used against them. Before modern times, most armor was laboriously fashioned and elaborate, reflecting the soldier's importance and representative of his status.

Historical records indicate that many primitive warriors protected themselves with leather hides and helmets. For example, in the eleventh century B.C., Chinese warriors wore armor made of five to seven layers of rhinoceros skin and ox hides. The Mongols were using similar protection in the thirteenth century A.D. Thick multilayer fabric armor was another form of protection, worn by the Greek heavy infantry of the fifth century B.C. And quilted linen coats were worn by soldiers in northern India until the nineteenth century. The dominant Roman army outfitted their soldiers using a combination of fabric, leather, and metal, in addition to their weapons. After all, no soldier should go into battle unprepared. This preparation includes strategy, armor, and weapons.

As warriors fighting spiritual battles, we too must prepare if we're to rise victoriously over the enemy. Paul tells us,

> Therefore take up the whole armor of God, that you may be able to withstand in the evil day, and having done all, to stand firm. Stand therefore, having fastened on the belt of truth, and shaving put on the breastplate of righteousness, and, as shoes for your feet, having put on the readiness given by the gospel of peace. In all circumstances take up the shield of faith, with which you can extinguish all the flaming darts of the evil one; and take the helmet of salvation, and the sword of the Spirit, which is the word of God. (Ephesians 6:13-17)

Let's unpack this verse and learn more about how to use the armor and weapons God provides for us.

SESSION 1:
THE ARMOR

MEMORY VERSE OF THE WEEK

EPHESIANS 6:11
Put on the full armor of God, so that you can take your stand against the devil's schemes.

FIGHT WITH TRUTH

DAY 1

When you started the challenge, I wanted you to know what you could be. Now that you've surrendered to Christ and devoted yourself fully to following him, you're ready to take on the title of warrior. The reason you're now a warrior is that whether you know it or not, the moment you accepted Christ as Savior, you were drafted into a spiritual war. Salvation brings with it the freeing truth that we're now adopted sons of God; it also brings an assignment in the army of God. You're now under God's direction and protection.

Paul reminds us, "We do not wrestle against flesh and blood, but against the rulers, against the authorities, against the cosmic powers over this present darkness, against the spiritual forces of evil in the heavenly places" (Ephesians 6:12). Remember that as a warrior for God, you're an empowered soldier on a mission, fighting for a worthy cause. We value warriors for their ability to face fear and to persevere in the fight. Regardless of the possible outcome, warriors will forge ahead and do whatever's necessary to win the battle.

What the enemy always seeks to do is to make you forget who you are by feeding you lies. As Jesus says of him, "He was a murderer from the beginning, and does not stand in the truth, because there is no truth in him. When he lies, he speaks out of his own character, for he is a liar and the father of lies" (John 8:44). Because the devil knows that God is truth, his only resort is to lie. He's always distorting the truth to get you to doubt God's word and yourself. For this reason, you must constantly rely on the Spirit and his word to remind you of who you are in Christ.

Therefore, fastening on "the belt of truth" is the mental and spiritual way of acknowledging and readying yourself for battle. It's the first step a Roman soldier would take when putting on his armor. To live a victorious Christian life, you must first commit your mind to the word of God.

FX3 DAILY DIRECTIVE:

READ:
For we do not wrestle against flesh and blood, but against the rulers, against the authorities, against the cosmic powers over this present darkness, against the spiritual forces of evil in the heavenly places. - **Ephesians 6:12**

PRAY:
As you prepare to study, pray for the wisdom to understand and apply what you just read. Journal your prayer.

_____

_____

_____

_____

_____

_____

_____

MEDITATE / MAKE IT REAL:
How do I see myself in the passage(s) I just read?

_____

_____

_____

_____

_____

_____

_____

MEDITATE / MAKE IT REAL:

According to this passage(s), what am I called to do?

_____
_____
_____
_____
_____
_____
_____

How am I going to apply or do what it says?

_____
_____
_____
_____
_____
_____
_____

SHARE:

Share what you've learned with others.

_____
_____
_____
_____
_____
_____

FIGHT WITH RIGHTEOUSNESS

DAY 2

In Roman times, a typical armed soldier wore a bronze breastplate to protect his vital organs, primarily the heart. This breastplate was fitted with loops or buckles that attached it securely to the belt. If you recall, Paul calls this the belt of truth. Paul connects the two because if the belt is loosened, the breastplate will also slip off.

Without truth, we're exposed to attack. In addition, we can also commit the error of using the wrong breastplate—the breastplate of self-righteousness. Unfortunately, a self-righteous breastplate eventually leads to legalism or self-condemnation.

When Paul uses the term *righteousness*, he doesn't refer to a righteousness of our own, but rather to the righteousness of Christ. When we accept Christ as Savior, he issues the "breastplate of righteousness" to protect our hearts and souls from the enemy's attacks. We take off our worthless "self-righteous breastplate" and put on the one provided by Christ at salvation. This act of putting on is continual, and not a one-and-done deal. To put on the breastplate of righteousness means that we seek God and his righteousness above all else (Matthew 6:33).

Another way to think about this is that we're to pursue a holy life. Living a holy life means to separate ourselves from worldly ways. To live distinctly different from the world means that we reflect Christlike behavior.

To be clear, we're called to live not a perfect life but a holy life. Doing so requires consistency and commitment, as is well stated in these words from Paul: "Be renewed in the spirit of your minds, and…put on the new self, created after the likeness of God in true righteousness and holiness." (Ephesians 4:23-24)

FX3 DAILY DIRECTIVE:

READ:
*to put off your old self, which belongs to your former manner of life and is corrupt through deceitful desires, *²³* and to be renewed in the spirit of your minds, *²⁴* and to put on the new self, created after the likeness of God in true righteousness and holiness.*
Ephesians 4:22-24

PRAY:
As you prepare to study, pray for the wisdom to understand and apply what you just read. Journal your prayer.

_____

_____

_____

_____

_____

_____

_____

MEDITATE / MAKE IT REAL:
How do I see myself in the passage(s) I just read?

_____

_____

_____

_____

_____

_____

_____

_____

MEDITATE / MAKE IT REAL:

According to this passage(s), what am I called to do?

_____
_____
_____
_____
_____
_____
_____

How am I going to apply or do what it says?

_____
_____
_____
_____
_____
_____

SHARE:

Share what you've learned with others.

_____
_____
_____
_____
_____
_____

FIGHT WITH PEACE

DAY 3

Continuing Paul's analogy of the Roman soldier's armor, we come to the third essential element—the shoes. When I started to research this idea, I came across an inquiry where someone asked, "Why do soldiers wear combat boots and not sports shoes?" Although the answer seems apparent, the question behind this question is, "What makes combat boots so effective?" One contributor summed it up best: "Running/sport shoes are only made for a few hours on your feet and don't do diddly for your ankles, or keeping your toes from getting squashed or nails through your soles. Work boots, or combat boots, on the other hand, are made for over 8 hours on your feet, have slice, puncture, and crush protection, and keep your ankles from getting both cut up and turning, especially when you're tired or not paying attention."

Fundamentally, it's critical to have the right kind of shoes for battle. The Roman soldiers understood this, so they wore the *caligae,* or *calcei*. These leather "boots" were thick-soled and usually had multiple straps. Essential to the boot was how they fitted the underside with studs or spikes to dig into the ground or stomp on their enemies. In addition, this sturdy footwear protected them on long marches through rough terrain.

An important aspect of this analogy is that we, too, were once enemies of God (Romans 5:8-10). As a result, we were once subject to God's wrath and judgment. However, Christ took on the fullness of this wrath upon himself the day he died on the cross and gave us peace with God. Therefore we're now justified before God, through Christ (Romans 5:1). As such, God is now on our side, with us, fighting the battles.

Another term for this peace is reconciliation. We are reconciled with God because we are justified through Christ. Being reconciled with God means we now stand firm, knowing God is on our side.

FX3 DAILY DIRECTIVE:

READ:

but God shows his love for us in that while we were still sinners, Christ died for us. ⁹ Since, therefore, we have now been justified by his blood, much more shall we be saved by him from the wrath of God. ¹⁰ For if while we were enemies we were reconciled to God by the death of his Son, much more, now that we are reconciled, shall we be saved by his life. - **Romans 5:8-10**

PRAY:

As you prepare to study, pray for the wisdom to understand and apply what you just read. Journal your prayer.

_____
_____
_____
_____
_____
_____
_____
_____

MEDITATE / MAKE IT REAL:

How do I see myself in the passage(s) I just read?

_____
_____
_____
_____
_____
_____
_____
_____

MEDITATE / MAKE IT REAL: ☐

According to this passage(s), what am I called to do?

_____
_____
_____
_____
_____
_____
_____

How am I going to apply or do what it says?

_____
_____
_____
_____
_____
_____
_____

SHARE:

Share what you've learned with others.

_____
_____
_____
_____
_____
_____

FIGHT WITH FAITH

DAY 4

The Roman soldier used his shield both offensively and defensively. It was usually as large as a door, and would cover his entire body. He used it defensively when opponents came too close, and he also used offensively to push them back.

Also, when a group of fighting Roman soldiers—a phalanx—stood shoulder to shoulder, they used their raised shields to create an almost impenetrable enclosure around themselves, called a *testudo* ("tortoise"). In the movie *Gladiator*, when newbie gladiators first come out into the arena, they're each holding a shield, but they're frightened, scattered, and unsure of what to do. The gladiator Maximus (played by Russell Crowe) orders the men to group together to create a unified *testudo* to protect themselves from their opponents' attacks. Using his military experience as a commanding officer, Maximus then directs the men in how to fight. He knows that their shields will serve both as protection and as an offensive weapon.

We too must take up the shield of faith to guard ourselves against the fiery darts of the devil. The shield of faith is how we protect ourselves from the temptations the enemy fires at us from a distance with the intention to burn us, distract us, disperse us, and destroy us. Paul uses the analogy of the fiery darts because in those times, enemies would wrap their arrowheads with a clothlike material soaked in a flammable liquid. The intention was for their lit arrows to ignite an engulfing fire. That's a picture of how Satan tempts us and tries to harm us spiritually. Therefore we need our shield of faith. It's our steadfast and unshakeable confidence in God, his word, and his promises.

Not only is the shield of faith our first line of defense from temptations, but it's also how we push back and prepare ourselves for counterattack. Faith is also the act of making Christ first in your life. Making Christ and his word first in your life is fundamental, and a gift of the Holy Spirit (Ephesians 2:8-9).

FX3 DAILY DIRECTIVE:

READ:

Now faith is the assurance of things hoped for, the conviction of things not seen. [2] For by it the people of old received their commendation. [6] And without faith it is impossible to please him, for whoever would draw near to God must believe that he exists and that he rewards those who seek him - **Hebrews 11:1-2, 6**

PRAY:

As you prepare to study, pray for the wisdom to understand and apply what you just read. Journal your prayer.

_____

_____

_____

_____

_____

_____

_____

MEDITATE / MAKE IT REAL:

How do I see myself in the passage(s) I just read?

_____

_____

_____

_____

_____

_____

_____

_____

MEDITATE / MAKE IT REAL:

According to this passage(s), what am I called to do?

_____
_____
_____
_____
_____
_____
_____

How am I going to apply or do what it says?

_____
_____
_____
_____
_____
_____
_____

SHARE:

Share what you've learned with others.

_____
_____
_____
_____
_____
_____
_____

FIGHT WITH SALVATION

DAY 5

There's an old Japanese tale about a general of a small army who decided he would launch an attack against a formidable opponent. Outnumbered but confident that his forces could achieve victory, the general called his lieutenant and told him to ready the soldiers for battle. The lieutenant did as instructed and laid out the general's well-devised plan with the soldiers. However, sensing that they were outnumbered and overpowered, the men started doubting their chances of success and the general's plan. Regardless, the general decided to move ahead with the assault.

When the army started marching toward the battlefield, the general sensed the growing fear and doubt among his men. So he had them halt at a place to pray for victory. After the prayer, the general lifted a coin in the air and said, "With faith in destiny, I'll now toss the coin. If it's heads, we'll win; if's tails, we'll lose." He tossed up the coin, and when it landed back in his hand, it came up heads. Emboldened by the apparently guaranteed victory, the soldiers went off bravely into battle. They fought fiercely and boldly, eventually defeating the shocked enemy.

After the battle, the lieutenant, filled with confidence, said to the general, "As destiny showed us through the toss of the coin, we won the battle. This is proof that no one can change destiny."

The general smiled wryly, and took the coin out for the lieutenant to see. Upon closer examination, the lieutenant noticed that the two sides of the coin were identical. He then recognized the general's complete confidence in his army, even when the soldiers doubted they could win.

Unlike this story, God, the ultimate General, knows well and has complete confidence that our enemy will be defeated. As belivers, our assurance doesn't come from relying on destiny or chance, but rather on our omnipotent God.

FX3 DAILY DIRECTIVE:

READ:
Therefore I endure everything for the sake of the elect, that they also may obtain the salvation that is in Christ Jesus with eternal glory. [11] The saying is trustworthy, for: If we have died with him, we will also live with him; [12] if we endure, we will also reign with him; if we deny him, he also will deny us; [13] if we are faithless, he remains faithful— for he cannot deny himself. - **2 Timothy 2:10-13**

PRAY:
As you prepare to study, pray for the wisdom to understand and apply what you just read. Journal your prayer.

MEDITATE / MAKE IT REAL:
How do I see myself in the passage(s) I just read?

MEDITATE / MAKE IT REAL:

According to this passage(s), what am I called to do?

_____
_____
_____
_____
_____
_____
_____

How am I going to apply or do what it says?

_____
_____
_____
_____
_____
_____
_____

SHARE:

Share what you've learned with others.

_____
_____
_____
_____
_____
_____
_____

FIGHT WITH
THE SWORD

DAY 6

The Greek word for "sword" used in Ephesians 6:17 is *machaira*. According to Roman accounts, their *machaira* was a deadly compact sword used by the Roman soldier in close-quarter combat, and many times with a shield. Although the *machaira* could measure up to nineteen inches, it was often shorter and shaped more like a dagger.

Because of the *machaira*'s portability, most Roman soldiers always had one on their person. It was such a popular and effective weapon of self-defense that even Peter carried one. Scripture mentions Peter using a *machaira* when soldiers came and confronted Jesus and his disciples in the garden of Gethsemane (John 18:11). Emboldened by Jesus's power to "drop" these soldiers to their knees just by pronouncing his name (18:4-6), Peter brandished his sword and ended up cutting off a soldier's ear. This event portrays how we, too, have a powerful *machaira*, but it's only as effective as the one who wields it.

Scripture describes itself as the *machaira* of the Spirit. Like the Roman soldier's sword, we use the word of God both offensively and defensively. No reputable Roman soldier would dare walk around without his *machaira*.

In Luke 4 when Jesus is tempted, he fights the enemy with the powerful *machaira*—the word of God—and so should we. That's why we're instructed to "meditate on it day and night, so that you may be careful to do according to all that is written in it. For then you will make your way prosperous, and then you will have good success" (Joshua 1:8). This means we must read God's word, study it, meditate on it, and memorize it daily.

Like the Roman soldier, our *machaira*, the word of God, should be on us and in us at all times. However, Scripture is not a mere book we carry around; it's a living and active weapon we must use.

FX3 DAILY DIRECTIVE:

READ:
For the word of God is alive and active. Sharper than any double-edged sword, it penetrates even to dividing soul and spirit, joints and marrow; it judges the thoughts and attitudes of the heart. - **Hebrews 4:12**

PRAY:
As you prepare to study, pray for the wisdom to understand and apply what you just read. Journal your prayer.

_____

_____

_____

_____

_____

_____

_____

MEDITATE / MAKE IT REAL:
How do I see myself in the passage(s) I just read?

_____

_____

_____

_____

_____

_____

_____

_____

MEDITATE / MAKE IT REAL:

According to this passage(s), what am I called to do?

How am I going to apply or do what it says?

SHARE:

Share what you've learned with others.

FX3 DAILY DIRECTIVE:

READ:

PRAY:

As you prepare to study, pray for the wisdom to understand and apply what you just read. Journal your prayer.

_____
_____
_____
_____
_____
_____
_____

MEDITATE / MAKE IT REAL:

How do I see myself in the passage(s) I just read?

_____
_____
_____
_____
_____
_____
_____

DAY 7

MEDITATE / MAKE IT REAL:

According to this passage(s), what am I called to do?

How am I going to apply or do what it says?

SHARE:

Share what you've learned with others.

SESSION 2:
THE WARRIOR WAY

MEMORY VERSE OF THE WEEK
I TIMOTHY 4:7
Have nothing to do with irreverent, silly myths. Rather train yourself for godliness;

A few years ago, I had the privilege of meeting one of the most inspiring men in my life. I almost missed out on meeting him, but providentially, we ended up connecting. He goes by the name Drake, and we met while he was spearheading a citywide ministry outreach. After his presentation, I felt a need to connect with him and learn more about this man. Something about his persona resonated with me.

Afterward, we struck up a conversation that eventually led to our getting together over lunch. In time, that initial meeting turned into a friendship that continues to strengthen today.

One of the things my buddy Drake excels at—and which I admire most about him—is his self-discipline. As far as I know, Drake has always been goal-driven and athletic. Whether it was playing football and running track at Samford University in Birmingham, Alabama, or winning the Warrior Dash (one of the most grueling 5K mud-run obstacle races on the planet), or competing in CrossFit Games, or representing Team USA on Netflix's *Ultimate Beastmaster*, Drake always gives it his best. He trains incessantly and prepares methodically for every endeavor he undertakes.

In addition to being a competitive athlete, Drake is also a husband of sixteen years to Heidi, and a father of four. He's a certified fitness instructor, an entrepreneur, a director for the Cru ministry organization, and a pastor. He's passionate about helping people transform their lives. What's most amazing is that he accomplishes all these things—and so much more—despite being diagnosed with multiple sclerosis.

When asked about how this disease has affected his outlook on life, he said, "After some time of wrestling with uncertainty, I came to realize that only God knows what the future holds. My family had a saying growing up that always stuck with me: 'Yesterday is history, tomorrow is a mystery; all we have is today—and it's a gift, which is why it's called the *present*.' Once I accepted this reality—that each day was truly a gift, and it was all I had—I wanted to invest my time wisely."

THE WARRIOR WAY
THE WARRIOR CODE

DAY 8

Throughout history, warrior cultures from various areas and cultures of the world have constructed codes of behavior based on an ideal image of what a warrior is. From the ancient Greeks and Romans to Vikings and Celts, and from medieval knights to Native American tribesmen, warrior cultures have always sought to live by a rule of expected conduct and ideals. Some of these codes are passed down only orally. At other times, they're expressly written. Regardless of how they're passed on, their goal is always the same: to hold a warrior to a higher standard than what's required for the ordinary citizens he serves. These codes also define how warriors should interact with their comrades, especially in helping to hold each other accountable.

In an essay on ideals of the warrior code down through history, ethics professor Shannon E. French states that the warrior's code is a shield that guards the warrior's humanity. "When there are no codes, innocents—those least able to defend themselves—become easy targets for atrocity."

She recounts the legend that when a Spartan mother sent her son off to war, she would tell him, "Come back with your shield—or on it." To come back without his shield meant that the warrior had laid it down to break ranks and run from battle. His shield was meant to protect not only himself but also the man next to him in formation, so dropping or leaving behind his shield would show that he was a coward who broke faith with his comrades. However, to come back *on* his shield meant that he was mortally wounded or already dead, thus demonstrating adherence to the code of "death before dishonor," fighting to the end with one's honor intact.

In the spiritual warfare that confronts every Christian man, he must forge ahead and do whatever's necessary to win the battle while living according to scriptural truth. These FX3 Warriors live according to different standards and expectations, something beyond what is natural or common. These standards or tenets are *Faith Fire Fury*.

FX3 DAILY DIRECTIVE:

READ:
Blessed be the Lord, my rock, who trains my hands for war, and my fingers for battle; ² he is my steadfast love and my fortress, my stronghold and my deliverer, my shield and he in whom I take refuge, who subdues peoples under me.- **Psalm 144:1-2**

PRAY:
As you prepare to study, pray for the wisdom to understand and apply what you just read. Journal your prayer.

_____
_____
_____
_____
_____
_____
_____

MEDITATE / MAKE IT REAL:
How do I see myself in the passage(s) I just read?

_____
_____
_____
_____
_____
_____
_____
_____

MEDITATE / MAKE IT REAL:

Write and recite the three FX3 Tenets:

_____
_____
_____
_____
_____
_____
_____
_____

How am I going to live according to the three tenets?

_____
_____
_____
_____
_____
_____
_____
_____

SUPPLICATION:

Pray for strength and perseverance to follow through in obedience. Journal your prayer.

_____
_____
_____
_____
_____
_____
_____

THE WARRIOR WAY
THE WARRIOR MINDSET

DAY 9

By now you've heard me many times say: *You were made to be a warrior.* There are two parts to this statement.

The first is, "You were *made...*" No one is simply born a warrior. Much like our natural birth, we don't come into this world with all the knowledge, training, armor, or weapons to be a warrior. Instead, we're born as a babe—defenseless and drinking milk. This "drinking milk" analogy is how Scripture refers to those who aren't yet mature in faith and righteousness (Hebrews 5:13). Maturing both physically and spiritually takes time, and it happens in stages or phases. It's a journey with the long game in mind. There's no way to rush this process.

The second part of my statement is "...a warrior." A warrior is what God made you to be—more specifically, a godly warrior. The godly warrior is a man who lives under God's authority in order to be transformed by God into the likeness of his Son. This process of sanctification is accomplished through the Spirit, but also requires an effort on our part. I don't mean to imply that we, on our own, can achieve Christlikeness. Rather, "our part" consists of acting in faith and obedience under the Holy Spirit's authority to do the work in us.

Therefore, the warrior mindset is how the godly man continually works to grow spiritually and to live under the Spirit's authority. To achieve this growth and quality of life, a warrior must practice what I believe are the four fundamental spiritual disciplines:

Reading, studying, and meditating on God's word (2 Timothy 3:16-17);

Praying (Ephesians 6:18);

Fellowship with other believers (Hebrews 10:24-25); and

Witnessing to the world (Matthew 28:19).

FX3 DAILY DIRECTIVE:

READ:
Have nothing to do with irreverent, silly myths. Rather train yourself for godliness; [8] for while bodily training is of some value, godliness is of value in every way, as it holds promise for the present life and also for the life to come. - **1 Timothy 4:7–8**

PRAY:
As you prepare to study, pray for the wisdom to understand and apply what you just read. Journal your prayer.

_____
_____
_____
_____
_____
_____
_____

MEDITATE / MAKE IT REAL:
How do I see myself in the passage(s) I just read?

_____
_____
_____
_____
_____
_____
_____
_____

MEDITATE / MAKE IT REAL:

According to this passage(s), what am I called to do?

_____
_____
_____
_____
_____
_____
_____

How am I going to apply or do what it says?

_____
_____
_____
_____
_____
_____
_____

SHARE:

Share what you've learned with others.

_____
_____
_____
_____
_____
_____

THE WARRIOR MINDSET
THE WORD

DAY 10

In the year 1808, an American seal-hunting ship happened upon an isolated island in the South Pacific. When crew members rowed ashore, they made an astounding discovery. The island was populated by descendants of the men who had perpetrated the infamous "mutiny on the *Bounty*" nearly two decades earlier.

One of the mutineers—Jack Adams—was still alive, and he had an amazing story to tell. After burning the HMS *Bounty* in a bay alongside the island, the unruly mutineers (along with their Polynesian wives and mixed-breed children) had settled into an existence of unrestrained debauchery, disease, and disorder.

Adams told of how alcoholism, murder, disease, and other health problems had taken the lives of most of the mutineers. But Adams and one other shipmate became ashamed of the violence and horrors they'd witnessed and been a part of. Adams told how the two of them had repented and felt a deep need to begin living according to biblical principles.

They began to teach the children to read and write, and more importantly introduced them to God through a Bible and a Church of England prayer book rescued from the *Bounty*. As a result, despite the horrific events in their background, the people were transformed and became a community noted for its exemplary morality."

What's particularly impressive in this story is how God's message of salvation by grace worked to transform murderous, criminal-minded sailors into peace-loving patriarchs, and a lost community of people into a virtuous generation.

Reading, studying, and meditating on God's word is critical for every believer. It's not enough to study and read it occasionally—it needs to be a daily discipline.

FX3 DAILY DIRECTIVE:

READ:
Be careful to obey all these words that I command you, that it may go well with you and with your children after you forever, when you do what is good and right in the sight of the Lord your God. - **Deuteronomy 12:28**

PRAY:
As you prepare to study, pray for the wisdom to understand and apply what you just read. Journal your prayer.

_____
_____
_____
_____
_____
_____
_____

MEDITATE / MAKE IT REAL:
How do I see myself in the passage(s) I just read?

_____
_____
_____
_____
_____
_____
_____
_____

MEDITATE / MAKE IT REAL:

According to this passage(s), what am I called to do?

How am I going to apply or do what it says?

SHARE:

Share what you've learned with others.

THE WARRIOR MINDESET
PRAYER

DAY 11

William and the Windmill is a documentary film based on the book *The Boy Who Harnessed the Wind* by the African writer William Kamkwamba. When he was a boy in a tiny village in the East African nation of Malawi, a terrible drought had struck, threatening the people with starvation.

But from science books, young William got the idea of harnessing the power of the wind to rescue his family and his village. By building a windmill from scrap material, they could generate electricity and also pump water. William's father had lost hope, and he viewed his son's idea as a waste of time and resources. Eventually, however, he conceded to help his son build a full-sized wind turbine. To everyone's amazement, the plan worked! Afterward, William produced more wind turbines and various other nature-powered devices to improve his people's quality of life. Today, William Kamkwamba travels the world, telling his story and inspiring others.

His story is a reminder of how we also need the life-giving power of the air or *pneuma*, which is the Spirit, to supply us the living water we so desperately need for our spiritual life.

This living water is the Spirit, and without it we'll eventually find ourselves weakened by a spiritual drought. We'll become unproductive and fruitless. Therefore we need to harness the power of the Spirit to get the living water flowing and keep it going. In addition to reading God's word, the other way to fight our spiritual battles—and to harness the Spirit's power—is through prayer.

One of the greatest privileges and honors we have is that of being heard by the creator of the universe. This includes communicating to him our deepest desires, our most grievous hurts, our sweetest joys, and our loneliest thoughts. We make ourselves heard through prayer, while also listening to God through prayer.

Prayer is one of the most powerful and yet most misunderstood truths in the Bible, but its power should not be underestimated.

FX3 DAILY DIRECTIVE:

READ:
Likewise the Spirit helps us in our weakness. For we do not know what to pray for as we ought, but the Spirit himself intercedes for us with groanings too deep for words.
Romans 8:26

PRAY:
As you prepare to study, pray for the wisdom to understand and apply what you just read. Journal your prayer.

_____
_____
_____
_____
_____
_____
_____
_____

MEDITATE / MAKE IT REAL:
How do I see myself in the passage(s) I just read?

_____
_____
_____
_____
_____
_____
_____
_____

MEDITATE / MAKE IT REAL:

According to this passage(s), what am I called to do?

_____
_____
_____
_____
_____
_____
_____

How am I going to apply or do what it says?

_____
_____
_____
_____
_____
_____
_____

SHARE:

Share what you've learned with others.

_____
_____
_____
_____
_____
_____
_____

THE WARRIOR MINDESET
FELLOWSHIP

DAY 12

Band of Brothers was a dramatized TV series based on the actual World War II accounts of "Easy Company"—the paratroopers of E Company, 2nd Battalion, 506th Regiment, of the 101st Airborne Division. The TV series follows the lives of these soldiers from their training to their deployments, and then on to their lives after the war.

The series opens with these men's paratrooper training at Camp Toccoa, Georgia, at the end of 1942. We see how the men forged a bond with each other, and deepened their commitment to excel as paratroopers. After completing their initial training, the men continued training at various military installations in the U.S. and overseas. All along, we witness their challenges and victories in working as a unit.

Throughout the series, the men deploy on various missions and engage in multiple battles. They face many losses and hardships during that time. However, what stood out for me is that despite these challenges, the men known as Easy Company developed a reputation as competent, disciplined, and committed soldiers who got the job done.

Not surprisingly, these were the same men who gained wide recognition as the "Screaming Eagles" of the 101st Airborne, known for their bravery and fortitude. Although these men were far from perfect, what was most significant was how they developed and deepened the bond between them. It was through this bond that they endured the battles and overcame what seemed like insurmountable obstacles.

This series taught me that battles are not won alone. The *Rambo* or *Commando* movies portraying the lone soldier defeating enemies on his own is just not true. The reality is that battles require the united efforts of many, under the leadership of a skilled commander. Therefore, in spiritual warfare, we must fight together under the leadership of Christ, not on our own.

FX3 DAILY DIRECTIVE:

READ:
And let us consider how to stir up one another to love and good works, ^{25} not neglecting to meet together, as is the habit of some, but encouraging one another, and all the more as you see the Day drawing near.
Hebrews 10:24-25

PRAY:
As you prepare to study, pray for the wisdom to understand and apply what you just read. Journal your prayer.

_____
_____
_____
_____
_____
_____
_____

MEDITATE / MAKE IT REAL:
How do I see myself in the passage(s) I just read?

_____
_____
_____
_____
_____
_____
_____
_____
_____

MEDITATE / MAKE IT REAL:

According to this passage(s), what am I called to do?

_____
_____
_____
_____
_____
_____
_____
_____

How am I going to apply or do what it says?

_____
_____
_____
_____
_____
_____
_____

SHARE:

Share what you've learned with others.

_____
_____
_____
_____
_____
_____
_____

THE WARRIOR MINDESET
WITNESS TO THE WORLD

DAY 13

Free Burma Rangers is a documentary film that follows the life and mission of David Eubank and his family. The Eubank family is an inspiration as they go through life following in complete obedience to God's calling. At every turn, they're met with life-and-death challenges that the enemy had intended to stir hatred and vengeance, only to see it turned to victory and strength.

During one impactful scene, Dave Eubank and his team of soldiers arrive at a location in Iraq where they encounter heavy enemy fire from ISIS militant soldiers. As they survey the area, they see dozens of bodies against a wall, all victims of genocide. Among the deceased are three children still alive. One of them, a young girl, is seen sitting next to her dead mother attempting to hide under her garment.

The rangers know that trying to rescue these kids without a plan and help could lead to imminent death for the children as well as themselves. Unsure of what to do, Dave prays. Coming into his mind is this verse: "Greater love hath no man than this, that a man lay down his life for his friends" (John 15:13). Dave asks, "You really want me to do that, God?"

"It's for love," is the response he gets.

"I don't want to do it," Dave replies. Torn by this request, he sends out a text to friends and colleagues around the world: "We don't know what to do. It's much more serious than anything I'd ever seen before."

At one point during the documentary, the interviewer asks Dave why he does what he does. With emotion, Dave replies, "It's right. It's love. It's God. Once you give your life out for love, you just want to be with this person again." He ends the interview by giving glory to God.

The Free Burma Rangers story is a testament to what it truly means to love others in complete obedience to God. To love others the way God loves us, we see them as precious to him, so precious that none should perish.

FX3 DAILY DIRECTIVE:

READ:
"This is my commandment, that you love one another as I have loved you. [13] Greater love has no one than this, that someone lay down his life for his friends. [14] You are my friends if you do what I command you".

John 15:12-14

PRAY:
As you prepare to study, pray for the wisdom to understand and apply what you just read. Journal your prayer.

_____

_____

_____

_____

_____

_____

MEDITATE / MAKE IT REAL:
How do I see myself in the passage(s) I just read?

_____

_____

_____

_____

_____

_____

_____

_____

MEDITATE / MAKE IT REAL:

According to this passage(s), what am I called to do?

How am I going to apply or do what it says?

SHARE:

Share what you've learned with others.

THE WARRIOR WAY
GODS FURIOUS LOVE

DAY 14

We're all familiar with God's fury as it pertains to sin. Those unfamiliar with God sometimes point to a God in the Old Testament who's angry, judgmental, destructive, unfair, hardhearted, and every other negative trait you can think of. When you read passages such as Jeremiah 4:4, Isaiah 63:3, Leviticus 26:28, Ezekiel 5:13, and many others, and view them outside their total biblical context, it would seem God indeed is all about avenging evil and sin with destructive fury.

Going further, the Hebrew term for fury in the Old Testament comes from the Aramaic word *chema*, which means anger or wrath. However, I'd like to attempt to further expand on this notion of God being a furious God. I say "attempt," because the more I learn of God, the more I realize we can't constrain or completely understand him with our limited intellect and insight. It's impossible to fathom the entirety of God. We can, however, meditate on what he has revealed to us in his word.

What I see is that the God of the New Testament is the same as he is in the Old Testament. The God of grace, love, mercy, sacrifice, and forgiveness is unchanging. Moreover, God loves us so passionately and intensely that he can't stand the evil and sin that comes between us and himself. He'll move heaven and earth to remove these obstacles so that we may be engulfed in his passionate love. I know of no other god who refers to himself as "a jealous God" when it comes to competing for our adoration and worship, but our God does exactly that (Exodus 20:5). Interestingly enough, The Hebrew word "jealous" in the Ten Commandments is *qanna*. It's used only to describe God, and is related to another word that means "zeal." Common synonyms for "zeal" are passion, enthusiasm, and fervor.

So there it is. God's fury applies not only to sin and evil, but just as intensely to his love for us. For this very reason, he sent his Son Jesus to die for us. G. K. Chesterton once remarked on "the furious love of God" in reference to God's grandness and awe in doing whatever it took to reconcile us back to himself.

FX3 DAILY DIRECTIVE:

READ:

No, in all these things we are more than conquerors through him who loved us. [38] *For I am sure that neither death nor life, nor angels nor rulers, nor things present nor things to come, nor powers,* [39] *nor height nor depth, nor anything else in all creation, will be able to separate us from the love of God in Christ Jesus our Lord.*

Romans 8:37-39

PRAY:

As you prepare to study, pray for the wisdom to understand and apply what you just read. Journal your prayer.

MEDITATE / MAKE IT REAL:

How do I see myself in the passage(s) I just read?

MEDITATE / MAKE IT REAL: ☐

According to this passage(s), what am I called to do?

_____
_____
_____
_____
_____
_____
_____

How am I going to apply or do what it says?

_____
_____
_____
_____
_____
_____
_____

SHARE:

Share what you've learned with others.

_____
_____
_____
_____
_____
_____
_____

SESSION 3:
THE FX3 BROTHERHOOD

MEMORY VERSE OF THE WEEK

JOHN 13:34

A new commandment I give to you, that you love one another: just as I have loved you, you also are to love one another.

On a December evening in 2004, in southwest France, a man named Jean-Luc Josuat-Vergès became depressed and went for a drive, leaving at home his wife and fourteen-year-old son. He took with him a bottle of whiskey and a handful of sleeping pills. He drove to an abandoned mushroom farm that had long winding tunnels dug out of the limestone hills. They spanned a length of five miles, with many blind corridors, twisting passages, and dead ends. Josuat-Vergès drove inside the tunnel opening, parked his SUV, and started walking deeper into these underground passages, carrying only a flashlight. But as he ventured further in, he became disoriented and lost.

As he turned down one corridor after another, he sank deeper into despair. Then the battery in his flashlight started to die. His once bright light dimmed, then finally went out. To make matters worse, he found himself bogged down in mud, which swallowed his shoes. Now barefoot and in the dark, he tried desperately to find an exit but stumbled and fell in the process. Eventually, he faced the fact that he might never find his way out.

Then, after thirty-four days, Josuat-Vergès encountered a miracle. On the afternoon of January 21, 2005, three local teenage boys decided to explore the abandoned mushroom farm for themselves. As they ventured into the dark corridor, they discovered the SUV with the door still open. Sensing something awry, they called the local police, who immediately sent a search team to the location. After searching for about an hour and a half, they found Josuat-Vergès just 600 feet from the entrance. When they found him, he was ghostly pale, had a long scraggly beard, and had lost about forty pounds. When asked how he survived that long, he told them he ate clay and rotten wood, drank water that dripped from the limestone ceiling, and sometimes even sucked water from the walls. He also recounted how at times, he got so desperate he devised a plan "in case things got unbearable." Fatefully, they found him before he reached that point.

Josuat-Vergès reminds me of how as men we also tend to retreat to a dark corridor or cave. We tend to run away to deal with our problems on our own. We have the mistaken idea that somehow, we can do it all ourselves. However, this isn't the way God made us. He made us as relational beings to have relationships—first with Him, then with others.

THE FX3 BROTHERHOOD
THE LONE WOLF IS A LIE

DAY 15

We aren't exactly sure where the term *lone wolf* originated, but over time it's become a mark of pride and honor. The reality, however, is quite different. Wolves are social animals that usually belong to family groups referred to as packs. Each pack consists of eight to fifteen wolves. Due to their organization and structure, if you ever see a "lone wolf," it's most likely the lowest member of a pack that has been driven out, which could happen for any of several reasons. But eventually, the wolf will seek a mate to start a new pack of their own. They never prefer to live in isolation—because they know it will eventually lead to death.

Years ago, I considered myself somewhat of loner. I was doing my walk with God on my own. During this time, I was a volunteer at my local church driving a van shuttling other volunteers from church to a remote parking lot. I did this for about two years, and spent most of my time alone driving the van. One day the Lord prompted me. It was time to move to a new church. My wife and I eventually found a new church. However, for almost a year I sat in in the pews listening to the service, then went home.

Then the day came when I was sitting in the service, and I was prompted to join a small group. The following week I met a great group of guys and a highly knowledgeable teacher named Jay. For almost a year, I participated, engaged, and found a renewed sense of belonging. In time, I came on staff part-time as director of men's small groups with the chruch. For more than a year, I oversaw men's small groups in the church, helped create and launch various programs, participated in church missions, and more.

The greatest reward throughout these years has been the friendships and fellowship with other godly men. These friendships and the fellowship have transformed my life to such an extent that my wife commented the other day how she was amazed at the number of friends and men I've both connected with and helped. This is all proof that this idea of the lone wolf is simply not true. Doing life on your own with no help from anyone is a lie from the enemy.

FX3 DAILY DIRECTIVE:

READ:

Whoever isolates himself seeks his own desire; he breaks out against all sound judgment. ² A fool takes no pleasure in understanding, but only in expressing his opinion. ³ When wickedness comes, contempt comes also, and with dishonor comes disgrace.
Proverbs 18:1-3

PRAY:

As you prepare to study, pray for the wisdom to understand and apply what you just read. Journal your prayer.

_____
_____
_____
_____
_____
_____
_____

MEDITATE / MAKE IT REAL:

How do I see myself in the passage(s) I just read?

_____
_____
_____
_____
_____
_____
_____
_____

MEDITATE / MAKE IT REAL:

According to this passage(s), what am I called to do?

How am I going to apply or do what it says?

SHARE:

Share what you've learned with others.

THE FX3 BROTHERHOOD
BROTHERHOOD

DAY 16

The movie *Hacksaw Ridge* is based on the real life experiences of Desmond T. Doss in World War II. The story focuses on how Desmond's beliefs forbade him from carrying a gun or threatening another human life. This belief is severely challenged when he joins the army, where he's initially ostracized by fellow soldiers.

As the movie begins, we see Desmond's upbringing and how this shaped his pacifist views. His father, an American veteran of World War I, grieves by the tombstones of his fellow soldiers who died in that war. Back home, he raises his sons in a pious setting and asks them to shun weapons. After Desmond nearly kills his brother in a fight, he reads the Bible and vows to never again harm another human.

After the boys grow up, and the United States enters World War II, the rigorous regimen of army training requires Desmond to successfully complete his firearms training. After a huge tiff with his seniors and with his father, an old corporal intervenes to save Desmond from being court-martialed by having him serve with the army as a medic.

Although Desmond is continually criticized by other soldiers, he finally earns their respect and adoration for his bravery, selflessness, and compassion in risking his life to save seventy-five men in the Battle of Okinawa. As a result, he becomes the first man in American history to receive the Medal of Honor without firing a single shot.

What impacted me most about this movie was the camaraderie that developed after the men witnessed Desmond's sacrificial bravery on their behalf. However valaiant, Desomond's story is more about how victory comes not from any one individual but from a group, a brotherhood. Fundamentally, a biblical brotherhood is a bond with others for a greater purpose. This week you will study the five reasons for being in a godly brotherhood.

FX3 DAILY DIRECTIVE:

READ:

And let us consider how to stir up one another to love and good works, [25] *not neglecting to meet together, as is the habit of some, but encouraging one another, and all the more as you see the Day drawing near.* - **Hebrews 10:24-25**

PRAY:

As you prepare to study, pray for the wisdom to understand and apply what you just read. Journal your prayer.

_____

_____

_____

_____

_____

_____

_____

MEDITATE / MAKE IT REAL:

How do I see myself in the passage(s) I just read?

_____

_____

_____

_____

_____

_____

_____

_____

MEDITATE / MAKE IT REAL:

According to this passage(s), what am I called to do?

_____
_____
_____
_____
_____
_____
_____

How am I going to apply or do what it says?

_____
_____
_____
_____
_____
_____
_____

SHARE:

Share what you've learned with others.

_____
_____
_____
_____
_____
_____

THE FX3 BROTHERHOOD
STRENGTH

DAY 17

After submitting my initial plans for a backyard pergola, the city denied the request for a permit based on a few requirements. The most critical element to receiving a permit was providing them wind load calculations for the structure. This request was out of my scope, so I reached out to an expert, an engineer, for help.

The term 'Wind Load' refers to any pressures or forces that the wind exerts on a building or structure. Living in one of the country's strictest code enforcement areas, Florida, it's critical to the type of storms we face. There are three types of wind forces that can affect a building.

The first type of wind load is uplift. Uplift is an upwards force of the wind that would affect roof structures or similar horizontal structures in a building, such as canopies or awnings. The second is shear wind load or the horizontal pressure or force that can cause walls or vertical structural elements to tilt or crack, causing a building to tilt. Finally, there is a lateral wind load. Lateral wind load is a horizontal wind pressure that can make a structure move off its foundations or overturn.

These wind load types affect the integrity of a structure and more so in Florida, where the weather may be extreme. For this reason, the city requests these calculations to ensure the design is up to the stresses it may encounter. More importantly, it will not only endure but stay standing.

This situation reminds me of how scripture warns us to be ready for the storms of life. It's not a matter of "if" but "when" and, more importantly, "how" and "why." The how is by anchoring our faith in the word and with the help of others. The why, so we may persevere and triumph over adversity. When we come together with our fellow brothers under the headship of Christ, we strengthen each other and make a significant impact in the world.

FX3 DAILY DIRECTIVE:

READ:
Bear one another's burdens, and so fulfill the law of Christ. ³ For if anyone thinks he is something, when he is nothing, he deceives himself. ⁹And let us not grow weary of doing good, for in due season we will reap, if we do not give up. ¹⁰ So then, as we have opportunity, let us do good to everyone, and especially to those who are of the household of faith. - **Galatians 6:2-3, 9-10**

PRAY:
As you prepare to study, pray for the wisdom to understand and apply what you just read. Journal your prayer.

_____
_____
_____
_____
_____
_____
_____

MEDITATE / MAKE IT REAL:
How do I see myself in the passage(s) I just read?

_____
_____
_____
_____
_____
_____
_____

MEDITATE / MAKE IT REAL:

According to this passage(s), what am I called to do?

_____
_____
_____
_____
_____
_____
_____
_____

How am I going to apply or do what it says?

_____
_____
_____
_____
_____
_____
_____
_____

SHARE:

Share what you've learned with others.

_____
_____
_____
_____
_____
_____
_____

THE FX3 BROTHERHOOD
COURAGE

DAY 18

As he finished loading the rented moving truck and his Jeep unto the trailer, he received a call from his new employer. Unfortunately, J.C's new boss stated he needed a specific paramedic certification before starting his new job. Somewhat disappointed, he decided to continue with his relocation plans.

At this stage, he couldn't go back. However, he and his wife still believed this to be a blessing. Now, it seemed, he would be living in Georgia on his own. They had invested their remaining savings in renting an apartment and all other expenses associated with the move in anticipation of his new job.

As he started the drive up north with his brother, he contemplated the months apart from his wife and kids and was concerned about passing the certification exam. Everything had occurred so quickly it was still a blur. Regardless, he pressed on. Then, about an hour into a twelve-hour drive, his brother noticed sparks coming from the towing trailer. Concerned, they pulled over.

When they pulled over, they realized the trailer tire was on fire. J.C. then immediately reached into his Jeep to pull out the fire extinguisher. Unfortunately, the fire extinguisher malfunctioned, and when he tried to get into his car to unload it off the trailer, he fell, injuring and burning himself.

The fire then climbed unto his Jeep; realizing they could do nothing, they watched as the flames consumed his beloved Jeep. He witnessed the years invested and memories made with the Jeep burn up instantly. Sometime later, I asked him about what helped him through the difficulties. He said that doing what God called him and the support of others gave him the courage to carry on.

His story reminds me of how there is no guarantee life will be easy-going and straightforward, even when God is guiding us. What is guaranteed is that God will be with us when we encounter trials and tribulations. He will also help you shoulder those difficulties with the help of others.

FX3 DAILY DIRECTIVE:

READ:

Whatever happens, conduct yourselves in a manner worthy of the gospel of Christ. Then, whether I come and see you or only hear about you in my absence, I will know that you stand firm in the one Spirit, striving together as one for the faith of the gospel [28] *without being frightened in any way by those who oppose you. This is a sign to them that they will be destroyed, but that you will be saved—and that by God.* - **Philippians 1:27-28**

PRAY:

As you prepare to study, pray for the wisdom to understand and apply what you just read. Journal your prayer.

_____
_____
_____
_____
_____
_____
_____
_____

MEDITATE / MAKE IT REAL:

How do I see myself in the passage(s) I just read?

_____
_____
_____
_____
_____
_____
_____
_____
_____

MEDITATE / MAKE IT REAL:

According to this passage(s), what am I called to do?

_____
_____
_____
_____
_____
_____
_____

How am I going to apply or do what it says?

_____
_____
_____
_____
_____
_____
_____

SHARE:

Share what you've learned with others.

_____
_____
_____
_____
_____
_____
_____

THE FX3 BROTHERHOOD
ENCOURAGEMENT

DAY 19

There's a story of how Menenius Agrippa, a famous Roman consul and general, once recounted a fable in an attempt to appease an insurrection of the Roman commoners. The issue was that people were growing agitated and angry at the continuous raising of taxes and decided enough was enough. Agrippa then told them the story of the "Belly and the Members" as it is now known.

The fable goes that once upon a time, all the limbs of a man's body became disgusted with the service they had to render to the belly. The feet and legs complained about how they had to carry the belly around. The hands complained about how they had to bring the food to the belly. The mouth complained that it had to chew the food for the belly. Every other body part made similar claims and complaints against the belly.

Once they finished stating their grievances, they all agreed they would do nothing more for the belly. However, shortly after they stopped working together, they found themselves starved and growing weak. Upon seeing this, they realized that they needed to work together for the greater good of the body. Agrippa then connected the story to them and told them that all ranks and states depended on one another, and they would fall unless they all worked together. So, in the end, they all came together.

Just like the band of soldiers in *Hacksaw Ridge*, eventually, they got past their differences. They focused on their collective purpose to inspire and encourage each other to accomplish something greater than themselves. These stories remind us of how scripture tells us that every believer has a purpose and plays a part in the body of Christ. God has gifted every one of us with gifts, talents, and resources to carry out His will.

When we come together with our fellow brothers under the headship of Christ, we strengthen each other to make a significant impact in each other's lives and the world.

FX3 DAILY DIRECTIVE:

READ:
Therefore encourage one another and build one another up, just as you are doing. [14] And we urge you, brothers, admonish the idle, encourage the fainthearted, help the weak, be patient with them all. [15] See that no one repays anyone evil for evil, but always seek to do good to one another and to everyone. - **1 Thessalonians 5:11, 14-15**

PRAY:
As you prepare to study, pray for the wisdom to understand and apply what you just read. Journal your prayer.

_____

_____

_____

_____

_____

_____

_____

_____

MEDITATE / MAKE IT REAL:
How do I see myself in the passage(s) I just read?

_____

_____

_____

_____

_____

_____

_____

_____

MEDITATE / MAKE IT REAL:

According to this passage(s), what am I called to do?

_____
_____
_____
_____
_____
_____
_____

How am I going to apply or do what it says?

_____
_____
_____
_____
_____
_____

SHARE:

Share what you've learned with others.

_____
_____
_____
_____
_____
_____
_____

THE FX3 BROTHERHOOD
ACCOUNTABILITY

DAY 20

The other day my son and I discussed responsibilities and our commitment to others. I asked him what made being responsible so challenging for him. After much consideration and thought, he said he wanted "freedom." I then asked him, "What does freedom mean for you?" "Freedom means being able to do whatever I want when I want. I don't want people nagging me or on me all the time." Afterward, I pondered his response and replied with a familiar expression, "freedom isn't free."

A song by veteran country singer John Anderson describes the price of freedom well:

I'm proud livin' in the U.S.A.
Land of the free and home of the brave
It might not be perfect but I'll take it any day
But how long will the eagle fly
And how many mothers have to cry
'Cause so many sons and daughters died
It's always been that way
'Cause freedom isn't free, it never was and never will be
What I'm tryin' to say there's always been a price to pay
Freedom isn't free it's been passed down to you and me
But how long will it be 'cause freedom isn't free
I said freedom isn't free

In essence, these lyrics remind us that there's always a price for freedom and that with freedom comes accountability. There's no better example of this than when Jesus died on the cross for us. He came to liberate us from the bondage of sin and death. This accountability means God expects us to live in complete obedience to him, his word, and sacrificially for others. He paid the price so that we may live freely with him.

For this reason, God will use you and fellowship with others to hold each other accountable for what he wants us to do.

FX3 DAILY DIRECTIVE:

READ:
David burned with anger against the man and said to Nathan: "As surely as the LORD lives, the man who did this deserves to die! [6] Because he has done this thing and has shown no pity, he must pay for the lamb four times over." [7] Then Nathan said to David, "You are that man! **2 Samuel 12:5-7**

PRAY:
As you prepare to study, pray for the wisdom to understand and apply what you just read. Journal your prayer.

_____
_____
_____
_____
_____
_____
_____

MEDITATE / MAKE IT REAL:
How do I see myself in the passage(s) I just read?

_____
_____
_____
_____
_____
_____
_____
_____

MEDITATE / MAKE IT REAL:

According to this passage(s), what am I called to do?

_____
_____
_____
_____
_____
_____
_____

How am I going to apply or do what it says?

_____
_____
_____
_____
_____
_____
_____

SHARE:

Share what you've learned with others.

_____
_____
_____
_____
_____
_____
_____

THE FX3 BROTHERHOOD
LOVE

DAY 21

A few years ago, Pixar released the kid's animated film, *Inside Out*. The general plot of this movie is about how an 11-year-old girl named Riley wrestles with anger, sadness, joy, fear, and disgust. Throughout the film, we see characters representing these feelings discuss how to process what's going on in her life. At different points, they argue, agree, and work together, all to help Riley make the right decisions.

Then, in one scene, all of the feelings collide and go on a wild and crazy "pin-ball" like adventure in her mind. During this process, she also starts creating new memories of her experiences. Eventually, the chaos subsides and returns to order when Joy and Sadness agree on each other's role in her life. Even though it's deemed a kid's film, it tackles many issues adults face. These issues are how external conflicts have a significant effect on dictating our internal state.

Although the film explores the human aspect of emotions and how feelings can govern our lives, it leaves out an essential factor as followers of Christ. Yes, God created us to feel and have emotions; it's part of being created in His image. Unfortunately, because of sin, feelings can also deceive us. Nevertheless, society is keen on telling us how we must do what "feels" right and that we should "follow our feelings." However, Scripture tells us to value obedience over feelings to follow God.

This film, is a stark contrast to the movie *Hacksaw Ridge* where we learn the demonstration of true, biblical *agape* love. Desmond decides early on that love will win out despite how fellow soldiers made him feel. Although he was ridiculed, ostracized, and persecuted for his beliefs, he didn't compromise, and he still found a way to fulfill his purpose and save save seventy-five of his brothers without firing a single shot.

We often don't feel like doing what God calls us to do, love others unconditionally, but rest assured that peace and strength will come from loving others as he loves us.

FX3 DAILY DIRECTIVE:

READ:
Love is patient and kind; love does not envy or boast; it is not arrogant [5] or rude. It does not insist on its own way; it is not irritable or resentful; [6] it does not rejoice at wrongdoing, but rejoices with the truth. [7] Love bears all things, believes all things, hopes all things, endures all things. - **1 Corinthians 13:4-7**

PRAY:
As you prepare to study, pray for the wisdom to understand and apply what you just read. Journal your prayer.

___

___

___

___

___

___

___

MEDITATE / MAKE IT REAL:
How do I see myself in the passage(s) I just read?

___

___

___

___

___

___

___

___

MEDITATE / MAKE IT REAL:

According to this passage(s), what am I called to do?

How am I going to apply or do what it says?

SHARE:

Share what you've learned with others.

SESSION 4:
REFLECT & REVIEW

MEMORY VERSE OF THE WEEK

I CORINTHIANS 16:13-14

Be watchful, stand firm in the faith, act like men, be strong. ^{14} Let all that you do be done in love.

REFLECT
WRITE DAILY DIRECTIVES

This week you will create your own devotionals. Each devotional should start with a journal, personal story, or insight. Afterward, you will select a verse or passage related to that writing. Finally, complete the devotional as you have in previous weeks using the RPMS methodology.

REFLECT
DAILY DIRECTIVE

DAY 22

FX3 DAILY DIRECTIVE:

READ:

PRAY:

As you prepare to study, pray for the wisdom to understand and apply what you just read. Journal your prayer.

_____
_____
_____
_____
_____
_____
_____
_____

MEDITATE / MAKE IT REAL:

How do I see myself in the passage(s) I just read?

_____
_____
_____
_____
_____
_____
_____
_____

MEDITATE / MAKE IT REAL:

According to this passage(s), what am I called to do?

_____
_____
_____
_____
_____
_____

How am I going to apply or do what it says?

_____
_____
_____
_____
_____
_____

SHARE:

Share what you've learned with others.

_____
_____
_____
_____
_____
_____
_____

REFLECT
DAILY DIRECTIVE

DAY 23

FX3 DAILY DIRECTIVE:
READ:

PRAY:
As you prepare to study, pray for the wisdom to understand and apply what you just read. Journal your prayer.

_____
_____
_____
_____
_____
_____
_____

MEDITATE / MAKE IT REAL:
How do I see myself in the passage(s) I just read?

_____
_____
_____
_____
_____
_____
_____

MEDITATE / MAKE IT REAL: ☐

According to this passage(s), what am I called to do?

_____
_____
_____
_____
_____
_____
_____

How am I going to apply or do what it says?

_____
_____
_____
_____
_____
_____
_____

SHARE:

Share what you've learned with others.

_____
_____
_____
_____
_____
_____
_____

REFLECT
DAILY DIRECTIVE

DAY 24

FX3 DAILY DIRECTIVE:

READ:

PRAY:

As you prepare to study, pray for the wisdom to understand and apply what you just read. Journal your prayer.

_____
_____
_____
_____
_____
_____
_____
_____

MEDITATE / MAKE IT REAL:

How do I see myself in the passage(s) I just read?

_____
_____
_____
_____
_____
_____
_____
_____

MEDITATE / MAKE IT REAL:

According to this passage(s), what am I called to do?

_____
_____
_____
_____
_____
_____
_____

How am I going to apply or do what it says?

_____
_____
_____
_____
_____
_____
_____

SHARE:

Share what you've learned with others.

_____
_____
_____
_____
_____
_____
_____

REFLECT
DAILY DIRECTIVE

DAY 25

FX3 DAILY DIRECTIVE:
READ:

PRAY:
As you prepare to study, pray for the wisdom to understand and apply what you just read. Journal your prayer.

_____
_____
_____
_____
_____
_____
_____

MEDITATE / MAKE IT REAL:
How do I see myself in the passage(s) I just read?

_____
_____
_____
_____
_____
_____
_____

MEDITATE / MAKE IT REAL:

According to this passage(s), what am I called to do?

_____
_____
_____
_____
_____
_____
_____

How am I going to apply or do what it says?

_____
_____
_____
_____
_____
_____
_____

SHARE:

Share what you've learned with others.

_____
_____
_____
_____
_____
_____
_____

REFLECT
DAILY DIRECTIVE

DAY 26

FX3 DAILY DIRECTIVE:
READ:

PRAY:
As you prepare to study, pray for the wisdom to understand and apply what you just read. Journal your prayer.

_____
_____
_____
_____
_____
_____
_____

MEDITATE / MAKE IT REAL:
How do I see myself in the passage(s) I just read?

_____
_____
_____
_____
_____
_____
_____
_____

MEDITATE / MAKE IT REAL:

According to this passage(s), what am I called to do?

_____
_____
_____
_____
_____
_____
_____

How am I going to apply or do what it says?

_____
_____
_____
_____
_____
_____
_____

SHARE:

Share what you've learned with others.

_____
_____
_____
_____
_____
_____
_____

REFLECT
DAILY DIRECTIVE

DAY 27

FX3 DAILY DIRECTIVE:

READ:

PRAY:

As you prepare to study, pray for the wisdom to understand and apply what you just read. Journal your prayer.

_____
_____
_____
_____
_____
_____
_____

MEDITATE / MAKE IT REAL:

How do I see myself in the passage(s) I just read?

_____
_____
_____
_____
_____
_____
_____

MEDITATE / MAKE IT REAL: ☐

According to this passage(s), what am I called to do?

_____
_____
_____
_____
_____
_____
_____

How am I going to apply or do what it says?

_____
_____
_____
_____
_____
_____
_____

SHARE:

Share what you've learned with others.

_____
_____
_____
_____
_____
_____
_____

REFLECT
DAILY DIRECTIVE

DAY 28

FX3 DAILY DIRECTIVE:

READ:

PRAY:

As you prepare to study, pray for the wisdom to understand and apply what you just read. Journal your prayer.

_____
_____
_____
_____
_____
_____
_____

MEDITATE / MAKE IT REAL:

How do I see myself in the passage(s) I just read?

_____
_____
_____
_____
_____
_____
_____

MEDITATE / MAKE IT REAL:

According to this passage(s), what am I called to do?

_____
_____
_____
_____
_____
_____
_____

How am I going to apply or do what it says?

_____
_____
_____
_____
_____
_____
_____

SHARE:

Share what you've learned with others.

_____
_____
_____
_____
_____
_____
_____

DAY 29

WHAT WERE SOME KEY TAKEAWAYS FOR YOU DURING THE PAST WEEKS?

DAY 30

WHAT WILL YOU DO WITH EVERYTHING YOU LEARNED? BE SPECIFIC.

MEMORY VERSES

Recite or write the following verses from memory (Phase 1):

SESSION 1: PSALM 139:14

_____
_____
_____

SESSION 2: 1 PETER 2:9

_____
_____
_____

SESSION 3: JOHN 8:44

_____
_____
_____

SESSION 4: ROMANS 5:12

_____
_____
_____

REVIEW & REFLECT: ROMANS 12:2

_____
_____
_____

MEMORY VERSES

Recite or write the following verses from memory (Phase 2):

SESSION 1: JOHN 8:32

_____
_____
_____

SESSION 2: 2 CORINTHIANS 5:17

_____
_____
_____

SESSION 3: EPHESIANS 6:12

_____
_____
_____

SESSION 4: ROMANS 8:5

_____
_____
_____

MEMORY VERSES

Recite or write the following verses from memory (Phase 3):

SESSION 1: EPHESIANS 6:11

_____

_____

_____

SESSION 2: 1 TIMOTHY 4:7

_____

_____

_____

SESSION 3: JOHN 13:34

_____

_____

_____

SESSION 4: 1 CORINTHIANS 16:13-14

_____

_____

_____

NOTES:

NOTES:

PRAYER REQUESTS:

PRAYER REQUESTS:

DAILY DIRECTIVE COMPLETION TRACKER

Below are thirty boxes to help you to track your progress.
After completing a Daily D:
1. Check off the box that corresponds with the day.
2. When you check off seven boxes, celebrate your accomplishment.
3. Remember, be persistent until you are consistent.

DAILY DIRECTIVES - SESSION 1

| 01 | 02 | 03 | 04 | 05 | 06 | 07 |

DAILY DIRECTIVES - SESSION 2

| 08 | 09 | 10 | 11 | 12 | 13 | 14 |

DAILY DIRECTIVES - SESSION 3

| 15 | 16 | 17 | 18 | 19 | 20 | 21 |

DAILY DIRECTIVES - SESSION 4

| 22 | 23 | 24 | 25 | 26 | 27 | 28 |

| 29 | 30 |

WELCOME WARRIOR!

You've just completed the FX3 Challenge! Completing this challenge is a phenomenal accomplishment, and your fellow brothers applaud you for your persistence to be consistent. You're now part of the brotherhood and part of something greater. This lifelong transformational journey just started, and we want to let you know that we're here for you.

WHAT'S NEXT?

Completing the FX3 Challenge is only the beginning. We're now going to charge you with joining an FX3 small group or, if led, start one of your own. We're also inviting you to join us in our mission to help others become fully devoted followers of Christ. For more information on small groups, events, and resources, visit: **https://faithfirefury.com.**

As always, I continue praying for your success and direction from the Spirit. I look forward to working alongside you for His glory! It's now time to live with **Faith, Fire, and Fury!**

Your brother in Christ,

Carlos F. Peña

Made in the USA
Columbia, SC
15 November 2022

70928384R00065